WHALE WALKER'S
MORNING

WHALE WALKER'S MORNING

New and Selected Poems

Michael Shorb

Whale Walker's Morning

Copyright © 2013 by Michael Shorb

Published by Shabda Press
P.O. Box 70483
Pasadena, CA 91117
www.shabdapress.com

Cataloging-in-Publication data on file at the Library of Congress.
Library of Congress Control Number: 2013942787

ISBN 978-0-9853151-3-9

Painting on back cover: "Summer Eucalyptus" by Myrna Shorb Todd

To my mother, Helen Thisted Shorb, and my poetry muse,
Judith Grogan-Shorb, my wife, and best friend with love,
devotion and gratitude for the inspiration they gave me.

ACKNOWLEDGMENTS

Some of these poems have appeared in the following periodicals:

- "$100,000 Tigers" appeared in *Ambush Review*, 2011 and *The Meridian Anthology of Contemporary Poetry*, 2012.
- "Ahura Mazda" appeared in *Pulpsmith*, Winter 1982 and *Pedestal*, June 2011.
- "Beautiful Women, Lonely and Passionate, Waiting For You To Call" appeared in *Big Bridge*, 2011.
- "Canoe People (Tierra del Fuego)" appeared in *Michigan Quarterly Review*, Fall 1977.
- "Crucifixion Nails Unearthed" appeared in *European Judaism*, 2011.
- "Cold Call" appeared in *The Rockhurst Review*, Spring 2011.
- "Dead Birds Falling From The Sky" appeared in *Poetry Salzburg Review*, Fall 2011.
- "Elegy For The Aral Sea" appeared in *Gargoyle*, 2011.
- "E-Mail From A Total Stranger" appeared in *Other Poetry*, 2011.
- "Entering the Water" appeared in *Kansas Quarterly*, Spring 1985.
- "Environmental Report" appeared in *Toronto Quarterly*, Spring 2011.
- "Escaping" appeared in *Beatitude*, 1979.
- "Farm Horses in a Full Moon" appeared in *The Cortland Review*, 2011 and *Willard & Maple*, 2012.
- "Galloping Horse Unearthed at Leitai, China" appeared in *Embers*, Fall 1983 and *Cosmopsis Quarterly*, Fall 2008.
- "God's Eye in Deep Space" appeared in *Edge*, June 2011.
- "Hearing Lennon's 'Imagine' on the Wrigley Beach North of Mazatlan" appeared in *Pilgrimage*, 2009.
- "History of Laughter" appeared in *Rainbow Curve*, Fall 2004.

- "I Heard the Tread of Hunters" appeared in *The Nation*, November 11, 1968.
- "It Fell To Me" appeared in *Poetry Salzburg Review*, Spring 2008.
- "Kindness of Strangers" appeared in *Rattle,* Summer 2007.
- "Lines in the Water" appeared in *Big Bridge,* Spring 2011.
- "The Man Who Killed For Love" appeared in *The Sun,* November 1987.
- "The Wildlife Graveyard in Taiwan" appeared in *Michigan Quarterly Review*, Summer 1991.
- "Tunes For Bears To Dance To" appeared in *Cortland Review,* 2011.
- "My Father's Garage on Christmas Night" appeared in *The Sun*, March, 1983, in *A Bell Ringing in the Empty Sky*, Volume II, 1987, and in the anthology *To Be a Man*, Jeremy P. Tarcher, Los Angeles, 1991.
- "Names in a Jar" appeared in *European Judaism*, Autumn 2009, and *Names in a Jar*, Hood Press, 2007.
- "Plague of Lights" appeared in *Poetry Salzburg Review*, 2009.
- "Presidio Chapel, San Francisco" appeared in *Eagles of Light*, 2010.
- "Planet Sunburn" appeared in *Skidrow Penthouse*, 2011.
- "Preserve The Wild Horses" appeared in *East West Journal*, 1989.
- "The Rain Forest Massacre" appeared in *Religious Humanism*, Autumn 1992.
- "Strip Mining in Outer Space" appeared on *Accents, WRFL*, Lexington, Kentucky.
- "Time Capsule" appeared in *Pearl*, Winter 2010.
- "The Samoan Cookhouse in Eureka, California" appeared in *Poetry Salzburg Review*, Autumn 2009.
- "Uncle Sterry" appeared in *The Sun,* March, 1983 and *When Last on the Mountain*, Holy Cow Press, 2010 and *Journey,* Eden Waters Press, 2009.

- "Water Planet" appeared in *Friends of the Earth Newsletter*, and *Kyoto Journal 75*, and *The Great American Poetry Show II*, 2010, and *Carpe Articulum*, 2011.
- "Coal Mine Canaries" appeared in *Canary*, Hip Pocket Press, September 2012.
- "Whale Walker's Morning" and "The Wildlife Graveyard in Taiwan" appeared in *Michigan Quarterly Review,* Summer, 1977 and 1991. "Whale Walker's Morning" also appeared in *You Say. Say*, Uphook Press, 2009.
- "The Roman Soldier's Ear" appeared in *Queen's Quarterly*, Summer 2008.
- "The Dolphin Messenger" appeared in *The Sun*, Issue 81, August 1982, The Sun Publishing Company, Inc.

The publication of *Whale Walker's Morning* was made possible by the generous help of several people. As Michael's wife, I deeply appreciate and wish to thank: Teresa Mei Chuc, publisher of Shabda Press for her seeing the wonderfulness of Michael's poetry; Anne Valley-Fox for her editing the poems with such an "eagle's eye," and for making great suggestions; Myrna Shorb Todd, Michael's sister, for her beautiful painting and photograph. I would also like to thank Gene Berson, Steve Schutzman, and Neelie Cherkovski for reading the manuscript and writing such astute comments.

Judith Grogan-Shorb

CONTENTS

WHALE WALKER'S MORNING

Few records survive of the whale
walkers of the 19th Century.
Primarily American, with a scattering
of Dutch, Greek and
African, the whale walkers
based around the Boston-
Nantucket area
once numbered
  in the hundreds.

They counted Joseph's coat
the Minoan seed pearl and
the harmonica of the Indo-
European virgin among their lineage.

Unlike their leaner-
visaged brothers
  of the harpoon
they staked their eliteness
to light about the feet
ears tuned to a keening wind,
a finer sense of balance.

Of their concrete origins in
sea crossings, tribal dances and
the strut of mountain axemen
not much more is known.
Some have linked them to
rites among the Phoenicians,
gypsies of the Asian steppes,
to the tree at the edge of the world
in Nordic mythology, to intimates
of migration routes and open
country roads of earth.

Of whale-walking itself
a little more is known.
Both ancient oil paintings
and early brass-tint photographs
exist, though these provide
a dusty geometry of the total picture.

A few famous individuals—
        Nordo The Aborigine,
        Jack Clappe,
        Cave-bear Eddie
followed the practice of having
the first-walked whale
tattooed on their chest.

At any rate, reliable depositions
of the time attest to the
frequent existence of large
whale pods which made
hours of uninterrupted
whale walking possible.

The necessity of timing
whale walking sessions
to coincide with periods
just after early feedings
along migration routes,
coupled with the requisite
of near-perfect weather conditions
led to the adoption
of two popular
turn-of-the-century phrases:

"It's a whale walker's morning."

"A whale walker's morning
to you and yours."

2

Michael Shorb

SEA CHANGES

this drifting expanse of wind-
blasted ice is the new
PEACEABLE KINGDOM:
at night the hungry
polar bear and her cubs
creep closer to the fire,
the gasoline generator makes
rusty groaning noises,
above, cold brittle stars
populated once by goats and dragons,
turn away from us, offering
no advice at all.

THE RAIN FOREST MASSACRE

From Cancer to Capricorn
broken only by unmeasured
sea you once
stretched
       unfathomed
           gut of jungle earth
but man takes fifty
million years in his
hands like a mahogany
mill blueprint

and man is hungry to farm
and stretch out
       the pastures of his machines.
They say you
biomass and matrix
of unknown
plant and animal forms
shoulders weather rides on
genetic savings account
where the future of god resides
must be razed and infected

Bulldozed and harvested
Like some enemy
bird- and insect-headed
anathema to human kind.

They give you twenty-five years to live

Not caring what shape beyond that
Earth may take.

There is no
       Alexander of the Word

To unstring this knot
      or slash it free.

Somewhere at forest's edge
      a pair of macaws
Yellow beaks and blue wings
Luminous orange bodies
      flash in light
A moment and are gone.

      Only their beauty is real.

WATER PLANET

"The death of the oceans means the death of man."
-Jacques-Yves Cousteau

Now we've seen it
        from space:
green granite continents
rolling galaxies of charted
water salt depths
forging the birth and
death of man in a wet blur.

Despise what nurtures.
Take cyanide and dynamite
to coral, monofilament
drift nets to salmon and squid.

Repeat the
        'no-one's looking'
Anthem of the River Slavers,
bury waste and death
in the source of life.

Put the resurrection engine
of the world into overdrive,
harvest piled bones gone
to chalk on Antarctic beaches

Raw stone eyes
        of thalidomide bass
netted off New Jersey's coast
stare through tricolored haze—

A sea's no God
to endure everything.

Or is, and dies before us.

Dies with gliding dolphins
cast like leaves

hardens to a snow of petro-
chemical rosebud ash
            leaving only massive
tube worms and blossoming
magma rifts
on the deep sea's
desert floor.

CANOE PEOPLE (TIERRA DEL FUEGO)

They say this land was named
for hunting fishing
families who built camps
        in roan dusk
catching careless seals
gathering mussels
to roast over
driftwood fires
their stories scattered
on rocky ground
with leftover bones.

They say you used to roll
newborn babies in
the snow to teach them
strength, that clear waters
ran with meat, no need
for mining then
no Spanish princes
no clothes, no money.

They called you the Yahgans,
the Onas.
        The People,
you called yourselves.
The People.

Your flickering images reach
my TV screen showcased
amid commercials with
humpbacks mating
        in the Sea of Cortez
Solon geese hatching
        bronze eggs

in late November.

Sitting beside your haphazard
corrugated shack
        you tell interviewers
you do not believe
        in life beyond the grave.

They record your rare
        monosyllabic
love songs:
        to Kerrhprrh, parakeet
        painter of October leaves,
to Krren, the sun

to Kreeh, the moon
to giant sleeping mountains
        that once were human.

You sell small beaded canoes
to smiling cruise ship
strangers who lower
paper bank notes
down in baskets.

I can't even address your images
        to claim that some
        universal love unites us.

Or open a can of anything
without hearing
        the distant curses
        of your fathers
crying from the Spanish mines
        forced to dig tin
        in the fractured
        wakes of gold and silver.

Or fatuously contend
        that any system on
the over-managed earth
can save you.

Even the doors of knowledge
        are closed.

I cannot mouth the lyrics
from one of your droned out
legends of earth
        Fatherhood and sky
or reach out
        lost palms of my hands
        forming islands

include us, People, in your songs

we are dying too.

Michael Shorb

THE SAMOAN COOKHOUSE
IN EUREKA, CALIFORNIA

Crossing a bridge spanning
mud flats and salt expanse
we drive west from Eureka
to a dirt parking lot sparsely
populated with decal-bearing
RVs and foreign cars.

We enter the low log cookhouse
where lumberjacks from
South Pacific shores and northern
salmon-rutted coastal climes
once gathered
            around checkerboard cloth-
covered tables crowded
            with bowls of eggs
shingles of bacon
flap jacks piled on white plates,
coffee and the sweet, steaming
glue of berry pies.

Meals are freshly prepared,
anomaly in a fast food world,
and served family style
in a place as much
museum as restaurant.
            Guest register
filled with enthusiastic comments
about a need for multiple stomachs
and appetites bolstered by mirrors.

History room displays
crude amenities from birth
of logging age.

Primitive curling
irons, permanent wave machines
to transform women's hair.
The first thick-wired
telephone switching system.
Rusted gap-toothed saws
that brought a wilderness to heel.

Faded photo on antique night stand
shows everything:
old Ford logging truck
circled by grinning cutters, hats
cocked, arms around each other.
Behind motor and cab

a whale-sized tube of old-growth
redwood, rings running back
before measured time, before
Christ and Columbus, to unnamed
continent filled with untamed
rivers and trackless trees.

We can't blame these loggers
for their expressions of stunned delight,
for the hungry fire in their bellies.
They dragged their axes across
California: towns and cities
sprang like fireweed from the scars.
They seem as much children
at play as conquerors,
roaring in circles
from the Trinity Alps
through forests none could imagine
wearing thin, a taken-
for-granted bounty.

Exiting the Cookhouse, our stomachs full,
our minds reeling from a felled
heritage, cliched phrases fail.
Anger over diminished sanctuaries
for grizzly and spotted owl
is temporarily muted.

In harbor distance beyond parking lot
a Japanese container ship receives
cargo of clear-cut logs
spindly compared with
historical giants in
sepia-stained daguerreotype.

Rumors say these logs are buried on
beaches in
        The Land of Rising Sun
resurrection to take place
in some future time when

they will be the only giants left.

Fog and dense drizzle begin their
descent.
        We scurry for the warmth of
the car, return to Eureka.
Windshield wipers tick-
tock across the windshield.

Words do not come easily.

MAN BITES TIGER

News item: elderly Chinese merchant
found dead from overdose of ground
tiger testicles.

Lacking a harem, he began
frequenting prostitutes
on the dong dock
side of Hangchow.

Each night, after a daily
bread of Japanese electronics he opens
the numbered bag of dried
loin from #808
(or was it #208?) among
defunct registered Siberian
tigers rare as blue
snow lions in a pure land
Buddhist dream watching
his ragged yellow
gunner surge and stiffen
to a power stalk
too long for depths of wife or mistress.

Even the pros of Joy Street
learned to shun the tiger man
seeking the rapid gold of accountants
lacking such a swelling jungle baggage
pacing swinging solitary side-to-side.

At some point, no partner needed,
he began to sniff the vanished cat's
powdered crotch on lines
across a shell-
backed mirror like gray cocaine.

14

It was in this respect they
found him, empty mirror,
old wives tail and old
man, hard, member
waved at morning like a flag
and no tigers anywhere.

IT FELL TO ME

to express the confused
rage of the drowning
Polar bear battling
chemical winds and widening
water, its strength
exhausted by two hundred
miles of suddenly open ocean,
its mind unraveled by
the mystery of breaking
white ice canyons
teeming with easy prey
like ringed seals now vanishing

It fell to me to find
a calculus of the great creature's
final bellowing cry,
its final vision of glowing
cod and halibut slinking away
as it sank down
into cold darkness
it once had ruled

to find some explanation
for this vagrant,
unnatural sight:

colored waves dashing on leaden rocks

      a massive white pelt

floating.

ENVIRONMENTAL REPORT

Celebrating synapses of dubious
authenticity the upcoming
vote in the Congress of Clowns
heavily lobbied by well-dressed and
well-endowed slaves of
the meat and sugar industries—

Investment strategies are swept from
coffer tables of the rich and fatuous,
ground into floors of the Age of Reason—

Caught in the maw of global
warming the rabbit-eyed wetlands
shrink to a torrid vanishing point.
That's not fair in the witch's mirror
or the evaporating glacier
or anywhere else by the time
dusty African villagers starve and
the last light bulb for 100
miles flickers out—

But the sermon's been canceled in favor
of 24-hour barbecue and polar
bears smoke cigarettes in the shade
of Alaskan taverns and you,
if you carry a six figure
mortgage, watch yourself—

they're itching for a fight.

$100,000 TIGERS

Anything that can be
quantified and sold
can be destroyed,
even the barriers of habitat
won't save you, the warming
tundra leaking its methane
like any uninhabitable planet,
the immense bogs
brimming with hostile
insect nations, once
trackless forests
harpooned by roads, and thinning.
I can't even get a clear picture
of the exact tiger I'm talking about,
bounding through unseen
patches of snow, a riot of
predatory evolution,
synapses in perfect balance,
illuminating the half-
frozen blue shadows
of the Siberian forests they wander.
Now I'm casually informed
you'll be gone inside a decade.
Even the statement makes me feel
bloated, fat and human.
I'm told the gangsters who
run markets place a
value of $100,000 on your head.
They've got you figured out:
what the wonderful striped
hide is worth, the value of each bone,
each drained fluid, each vial of
dried-out hearts and livers,

each premium-priced
set of testicles,
most valuable, they say,
in the entire animal world.

BELOW THE PASSION RIVER STATION
(PETEN, GUATEMALA)

There's nothing there:
a trading post,
two bars hewn of rough-sawed
wood and corrugated plastic,
cerveza bottles
      iced in a metal tub
scrawny roosters
walking the premises
like shriveled kings.

An hour out by canoe
along the southern fork
of this misnamed river,
sun-drum and musty jungle shade
pulling us northward into
Peten's universe of green
distance
      clocked by one-celled
movement in shoreline moss
mud-flecked alligators
in Mayan slumber.

In the second-largest
rain forest of the hemisphere
we hike and crash,
      hacking through
fisted hunchbacked trees
crunching shells
      of nameless beetles
mocked by unseen
      howler monkeys.

Not even eight month seasons

of sheeting rains
flooding logging roads
can save this jungle.

Cedar and mahogany logs
come streaming out
like scaled giant fish
from salty interstellar depths.

Homeless tribes driven from
coffee fincas follow, fleeing
tired plots of grave-earth
to creep into the bounty
of Mother Forest.

So the Kekchi pray with firebrands
      of swaying motion
           to the jungle
                life they must ravage.

60,000 hectares
      vanish yearly
into settlements like
Sipens,
      a baked ash-
gray holocaust
of open space decked
by thin fields of scrabble
corn,
      huts propped on charred
logs,
      plastic sheets for windows.
Smiling children play in shade
as petty judgment
chokes inside my throat.
These gentle predators
are safe here for a shallow time

from social structures
from machine gun massacres
lice-scarred maize and
helicopter gunships.

Man cannot destroy
the force of life, burn
the pillars
        that sustain the world.

They know this as well
as any stranger

        nothing to say in any language.

They smile again
        thin fishers
sowers
        fathers children

from a stone oven smells
of corn become a deafening
song
        an evaporating cloud of love.

GHOST KING DRIFT NET, NORTH PACIFIC

Cut adrift 500 miles east
of Dutch Harbor this
Hiroshima
        of plastic thread
ghost king drift net
white wall of death
phosphorus seaman's trunk tumbling
past rock-starred

        Aleutian chain

along international date line
toward roots of Hawaii.

eighty miles of tattered blankness
preys on mid-migration
salmon, staring red perch

snags rusted car
        and redwood log
tennis racquet
        and crook-jawed
sperm whale —

what point naming
what it falls on

        drags in tangles up

falling through deep
space slate green

North Pacific

meteor of Taiwan
        fishing industry;

shroud
       market indicator

debit against the sea.

ELEGY FOR THE ARAL SEA

The river slavers,
their night's work done
move on from
dry Uzbekistan,
what was a robust sea
becomes a starving animal
of salt and sand,
90% dead.

Now in this newest desert
camels plod quietly,
passing abandoned
fishing trawlers
like evolutionary ghosts,
before them a vast plain
littered to the horizon
with dry brush and
the skeletons of commerce.

Winds carry this salted
stinging sand as far north as
Sweden and east to Japan,
but somewhere cotton grows
halfheartedly, buoyed by
diverted Amu Darya and
Syr Darya waters.

They still argue over dams
and hydroelectric projects
but the life is nearly gone,
at Muynak, once a bustling port
where net after net of twitching fish
were loaded, the deserted pier
stretches above gray

wasteland, like the last
stone arch in a ruined city.

Michael Shorb

THE MAN WHO KILLED FOR LOVE

You can't blame any
life on Mars for burrowing
deep in polar molecules
when your virtual fingers
come feeling around

Mr. Metal
Mr. Daily Planet
Mr. Praise the Lord and Pass
The Cherokee Removal

Your reputation's pretty well
shot on this island
roots and diatoms are prepared
to shrug you off like a virus
plutonium and wheat crouch
on the rainbow bridge threatening
suicide
          the buffalo tongues are gone

buffalo tongues you once
bolted down Saturday night with
black oak barrels of whiskey
while music soared
and dancers whirled

You and your deep love
for this planet are
touching everything

Everything's listening:

          dolphins and mice

quartz, rain forest parrots

air and ocean
currents, earthquakes and rain

They all want to hear another
of your famous torch songs

sing the one

where you

kill for love.

COLD CALL

Nobody invited me
that's the least
of my problems
I came limping in
to the harbor of
disenfranchised dreams
not expecting anything
willing to take a flyer
on the rest of history
rang the gong
outside your gate
just as the sun faded
disturbing you
just as you were
starting to make love
sitting down to
a favorite daughter's
wedding feast
how could I expect
you to open
to read anything
but pessimistic ranting
in the 'old mariner'
surging in my eyes?

You demanded a
toast in celebration
but I was selling
the usual serenade
of desperate animals

opening my overcoat
to reveal my
pocketed gallery
of shining disasters.

DEAD BIRDS FALLING FROM THE SKY

I'm already sorry
I brought it up,
lacking biochemical insights
I'm just another
slack-jawed singer in the chorus,
standing on a stage
meant for seers and prophets,
stammering my amazement,
refusing to perform
the math on this seeming plan
hatched by starlings and blackbirds,
dolphins and vanishing
forests of white western pine
(a degree or two,
turns out, means birds
migrate late and oceans of tiny
pine beetles prosper,
stripping life from slender trees).

Our destiny expands,
revealed in this maze of portents,
ice and fire and flood,
our dimly marked hieroglyphic
peers back at us
from jungle floor
and mountain vastness.

This is what we know.

OILY SEABIRD, EAST GRAND TERRE ISLAND, LA

It's an evolutionary
horror movie
in miniature
this one unrecognizable
seabird emerging
monstered by gushing
petroleum entombed
under the crust of the sea
beak to tail feathers
eyes staring out
nothing to do
when environment
alters abruptly
salt water turns
to toxic sludge
dooming you to die
standing on the same
beach as yesterday,
under the same reddening
gulf sky brooding.

ESCAPING

They weren't after me.

I wasn't the one tied
by the ankles to
a cyclops of uranium
dragged across floors
of the Age of Invention
a convict in chains
ram in the thorns
steel mill rabbit
in thickets of rain

they didn't hunt me down
in coal-
        black veins of my own land
smash the colored beads
of my alphabet
hook me across the gills
with a printing press
shoot me in some
neck of the woods
when nothing was looking

I'll see you around
drifting
        through town

soiled parody from
the Book of Prophets
blurting the old green songs.

last seed bursting
last wind stirring
last swordfish
        in slate-green sea.

PLANET SUNBURN

It becomes a joke before
we even understand it,
relegated to a kingdom
of cliché:
      the whole global warming thing—
it's that moment speeding
down a mountain road
when you realize
      the brakes are gone,
when you swim over and past
the shark net barrier
into darkening water—

the other morning in southern
Australia koalas staggered
onto public highways
in 120 degree heat,
begging passing humans for water—

the air crackled with heat
even after a flood of crows
rode the sun to the rim of distance—

as though nature was just joking around,
all those species about to go
extinct or insane only theoretical,
nothing to dry the moisture from your fields,
drain the animals from forests
and fish from the sea—

and you, every once
in a while, could just
write a check
or watch a special on PBS,
making everything all right.

THE WILDLIFE GRAVEYARD IN TAIWAN

Eleven lion heads and
skins in a shipping crate
ivory tusks sawed off
to feed the carver's
operations resettled from
Hong Kong, black bear
bladders by the gross and horn
of Sumatran rhino—800 left
$40,000 a kilogram destined for
the apothecary's pestle and
the shriveled loins of
Chinese businessmen.

What was basic fisher village
wilderness as short a time as
'46 ago is paved and populated
breathes with office window
lungs and beats with cold
gray CAD/CAM factory heart.

There are they say no
clouded leopards left to
roam the Chungyan and Shanmo
mountain spine of this
island jewel parting
Pacific Ocean and
South China Sea like
a swimming snail.

They used to roam bamboo-
flooded groves of arching
green but then went

down, into the accelerating
maw of those three intrepid
horsemen:
>hunting,
>farming,
>pollution.

Into the stockpile market
into the oblivion
of buy and sell.

STRIP MINING IN OUTER SPACE

The solution to our woes
hangs over us from
time past, stretching into
time future with glacial
precision, the stars are
an unfracked shale,
a mine shaft descending into
infinite utopias of energy.

Our future lies in the tools
we dream and invent,
at some distant point we'll herd
planets like cattle, sending them
down a chute to be de-
constructed of fauna and
flora and mineral essence.

For now, undeveloped, we only
dream of strip mining outer space
to warm our billions of hearths
and thousands of gleaming cities,
just give us enough time,
and smart enough machines,
we'll figure things out,
any disruptions due to
destruction will certainly
be a momentary inconvenience.

TIME CAPSULE

It had something to do
with global warming
anyway sand-
storms covered
badlands of northern
California somehow leaving
one of my poems as
a marker in time
excavated years later
it provided a contrast
to the official national
capsule back east.

Fortunately the buried poem
was quite an epic
anthropologists hefted out
so many crates of evidence
they resembled a line of
army ants.

We fared much better
than empires represented
by shards of pottery alone.

The crates ran from A
for Apple iPod to
Z for Zoroastrian creation myths.

It was all there:

    why we lived

    what we meant

    that sort of thing.

CRUCIFIXION NAILS UNEARTHED

They hold out these
gnarled rusted three
inch digits, one bent
upward, claiming
these once invaded
the abused carpenter's
bleeding hands.

Might we search the nails,
combing for the DNA
of Christ and the inner
watchworks of love, given with
such tender ambivalence?

Or would we only find
another testimony
of our enduring brutality,
gleaned where
the ancient
            hammer struck?

Michael Shorb

LINES IN THE WATER

Over coffee and time cards, we talk
Of lines in the water, salt
Eating into veins of world's
Rivers, saline encroachment,
Parcher of roots stuffing the Amazon's
Mouth
        pushing back lifelines
Of Aswan-choked
Nile delta
Torrents of Columbia
Crowded with dams
Clouded with wood pulp.

"Gonna fuckin' happen here," says Ben,
Ex-Navy, foreman.
        "Divert good mountain
Water down this Peripheral Canal,
Heist the balance, you'll see winter
Runs of salmon up the Sacramento
Go, you'll see the brackish
Sump they serve up for
Wetlands and a bay."

Lines in the water
        carry us back
To Shanghai, China.

        Oleg, emigre office manager

Whose parents fled Moscow in '17,
Following ice railroads
To Manchuria
        south and coastward
Across the Yellow Sea.

And Ben, a nameless face
In the victory fleet.
I am there in the listening.

Past Okinawa the blue Pacific
Mass sweeps green by
The East China Sea
To Shanghai, where sediment,
Russet breath of distant
Mountains
        fogs the Yangtze-Kiang's
Flowing, a line bends
In sea where the mud-

Flecked river's strength is spent,
Dull gold band streaking
        to deeper hues.

Ben looks up from
A half-packed bearing, rests
One hand on his bench, remembering:

"Called 'em the Garbage Chute Wars.

We were anchored mid river
On the Hangchow side, in '46.
Chinks would have little battles
Down on the water, maneuvering
Sampans for the territory
Right under the galley chute
Where the garbage dropped."
He chuckles, as much in resignation
As cruelty, a witness.

"They'd be down there,
        bloody as pirates,
Whacking each other

With jagged stubs of oar,
Muscling their curving
Boats into line.
    Damn cooks'd watch, drag
A barrel filled with latrine water
To the edge and

    BANG it'd bust

That fuckin' sampan
Poor bastards'd fly fifty yards,
Pigtailed rockets
    over muddy water.

They were starving, after the war," he adds,
Changing tones on a slight pause.

"Got that right.
Last months before the
Reds took over you needed
A wheelbarrow full of money
To buy a few apples
And a bar of soap,"
    says Oleg.

"I had a fortune once,
Printed on tissue,
    worthless."

He tells us about the Jesuits
In Shanghai St. Joseph's, how he
Memorized Geologic Ages to escape
Whipping
    with a leather strap.
About saving Troy ounce
Gold bars to bribe
    Japanese soldiers

As a clerk in the customs
House, accepting cumshaw,
    bribes of fruit and rice
Plying angled, pungent streets
With bags of walnuts from
    the orchards of Hangchow
While he lived upstairs by an ivied
Wall near the harbor where navy
Cooks laughed down on
Sampans bearing
    triumphant, starving men.

"This country's a Moneysaurus," Oleg laughs,
"I've seen it happen.
Big green thing strutting
Around now, but things'll change.
Things'll get it.
Climates grow dark.
Other animals'll eat its eggs,
Pick over its bones.

They'll fight like wild dogs someday
For eyeglasses
    car jacks and shoelaces.
The world's meaner than it was."

"Listen to you,
Old bastard,
Fuckin' prophet,"
Ben snorts, walking away.

But later, as I say good night,
Ben says nothing,
    gray head down
Staring across the deck
Of his wrench-strewn bench.

PLAGUE OF LIGHTS

They trusted us,
the animals and insects
seeking as we
to crawl and fly
from darkness.

As our cities expand
and the light intensifies
there is a bigger price to pay
than the shrouding of stars.

Polarized light from
the dark glass of our skyscrapers
is mistaken for
a beacon of water.

A reverse lighthouse effect
draws these small ones
to a gasping doom and I,
wedded to the same
plague of lights as you,
must take my place
in this chain,
following the lead
of turtles and dragonflies.

HISTORY OF LAUGHTER

The woman's voice
was trapped inside
the River Kronos,
it clung to silt and fish glide,
moth in torrential distance.

It was Old Winter himself
who intervened,
fishing the stiff voice out.

You owe me, he said, half
your love poured on stones.

We'll call it laughter.

Michael Shorb

BEAUTIFUL WOMEN, LONELY AND PASSIONATE, WAITING FOR YOU TO CALL

We men are looting
the earth in order
to stay erect,
freeze-dried loin of tiger,
ground elk antler,
horny goat weed
bolstered by plutonium,
pheromones of a barnyard bull and
yes, they call the biceps
'guns'

BEAUTIFUL WOMEN, LONELY AND
PASSIONATE, WAITING FOR
YOU TO CALL

And now our featured animation:
Mr. Potter from
It's A Wonderful Life and
Mr. Burns from *The Simpsons*
swim and cavort in an indoor
pool filled with Viagra tablets

BEAUTIFUL WOMEN, LONELY AND, WAITING FOR
YOU TO CALL

Hanging with my new friends
morning wood and Mr. Johnson
smoking this cigar,
sipping that cognac,
all women spread out before me,
electronic menu of harem eyes
breasts and thighs inviting

as sleep in a strange bed,
slippery strength of skin,
petal storms of completion.

BEAUTIFUL WOMEN, LONELY AND
PASSIONATE, WAITING FOR
YOU TO CALL

We men are stripping
the earth for profit,
let's talk it over on TV,
let's memorize the
rules that apply,
these are days when
they poison the lake going
for the gold, killing every
swimming thing, but agree
to repopulate it later,
days when they simply
cut off the tops of mountains
for easy access to rich
black seams of coal,
dumping toxin-laced
rubble into valleys below.

So sue us.
We're the fucking human race.
We do whatever we do.

BEAUTIFUL WOMEN, LONELY AND, WAITING FOR
YOU TO CALL

PRESERVE THE WILD HORSES

The last ranchers hold a newspaper
Gracelessly
     as prices fall
Their sheep and steers
Show panicky ribs to the desert sun
Wallow bleating and braying
In muddy skeletons of water places.

They cannot parachute the butcher down.
They cannot crane the lost meat skyward.
They can't prevent the wild horse
From drinking
     can't reason mustang and mare
Onto column inches of a reservation
So they roar out to trade in death (old servant,
coughing in glade of doom death) that served
The red-stained bison people so efficiently.
Ways of life and modes of nourishment
Aside for a century I swear let burger-
Glyphics and gas pumps grow dormant
Let rice sky and wheat
Be kings, let us learn
Everything we cannot know
But preserve the wild horses.

I cannot sculpt this feeling into reason.
Nature is not a piece of chalk
To scribble blunt or rope to throw.

The wary, timeless stallion
Pausing on a ridge, cocking ears to run
Carries my ability away, over
The dry hills,
to love freedom.

THOUSAND POUND WHITE STURGEON
DISAPPEARS FROM THE KOOTANI RIVER

How deep this root is,
stretching into jurassic
depths, sliding into
veins of the birth of rivers.

You couldn't break
the brotherhood of this river and
the long-snouted, armored
fish longer than a dingy,

not if you had a million years,
not if you flailed the water's
surface with the shards of comets—

Now more water's released
from dams, a brief penance
designed to placate the web of life,
summoning a further generation of giants
from green and murky depths.

"We hope," stated an official,
"to stave off extinction."

By this, of course, he referenced
the white sturgeon
long since gone.

E-MAIL FROM A TOTAL STRANGER

dear distinguished friend
since I am South African
since I've suffered from elfin grot
since childhood and now
find my prospects walking
along alone burdened
by four hundred million
dollars stolen from oil companies
I beseech your generosity
allowing me to designate you
recipient of this ill-
starred fortune on strict condition
that you distribute the cash
to sea lions and snow leopards
I only thank the common
Lord that this bond
exists between us
two human voyagers realizing
the sky is never red at morning
without a showering of fortune
no doubt you have divined
my need for a leather case
fitted with silver
to facilitate my hand delivery
personally to you
this virile sum in the name
of Christ our founder
so remit only the small
amount of eight thousand
four hundred dollars
let's make the sun

beating down on us
proud and remember
at all times the snow leopards

are counting on you.

Michael Shorb

THE CAVE PAINTER'S DEPOSITION

Should I say a river
met the wide blue sea
beneath a giant arch
of water-sculpted granite,
to say we settled this valley
by destiny or design
is falsehood, we were
dancing the fire and
skinned game end
of the day dance
we needed to stay alive,
we held our breath,
struck the earth
with a seed of future cities
in this place and not another,
and just to keep things straight,
I once ran with the hunters
before shattering this leg
I drag now, down
the dry black throat
of this cave, burdened
with a hide bag of charcoal
implements and chunks of raw
color coaxed from loam,
searching for just such a
sudden grotto canvas in
rock walls unseen by man.

You'd know the place right away,
the hushed air, a falcon of
updraft bearing away smoke,
at first I barely knew
what to do, scratched lines

53

became solitary elk on
river cliffs, a grazing herd of horses
came alive with umber manes
and wild blue eyes, bears
lumbered into the shadows,
looking back in alarm.

I had to talk fast
back at the campfire that night,
describing the paintings below
became the first song,
my agitated tapping on
stone the first music,
some wanted to kill me off
as an extra mouth to feed,
most wanted me around
for potential good luck
whatever they voted
to call me,
I might have been the first artist,
or the first priest,
or the first insurance agent,
yet became the first showman,
leading guided tours
of the hidden animal galleries
of my own creation.

BEAUTY

At Chauvet, sea-
changes drummed while
the father of artists
slathered pigments on
the blackened throats of caves

stick figure hunters
held their breath in
Paleolithic dawn

amber deer and yellow-
horned oxen
bristling in herds
bears and rainbows
beckoning

a century was nothing

a word crept forth, useless

it was only beauty

we longed for.

GOD'S EYE IN DEEP SPACE

We only call it
by this lofty appellation
to assuage our sense
of being utterly,
terminally alone

so it seems this utter
distance of gas and elements
slashed white across
deep space
            accentuated
by flares and
splashes of pulsing color
looks back at us,
returns our fervent gaze,
provides a reservoir
of hope however shallow,
at least, we can say,
these bodies
of bright water exist
vast distances away,
unreachable until some
future time.

NAMES IN A JAR

Sometimes all Irena Sendler
Remembered was a detail:

The names of the children written
On scraps of paper, buried in two
Jars in a neighbor's back yard.

97 now, she wheels toward a
Patch of sunlight in the
Nursing home recreation room,
Sits there all afternoon,
Rooted like a river oak.

She and some friends had smuggled
Jewish children from the
Warsaw ghetto in those days,
Sometimes in large black purses,
Sometimes in baskets covered
With blankets, slipping under
The eyes of the German guards
Like fish sliding beneath a net.

When the Gestapo caught up with her,
All they wanted was the names,
The torture would stop, they informed her,
When she gave them the names.
When her flesh seared and her
Thick Polish body registered
Waves of pain she came right to
The edge of madness once,
Seeing the interrogators as
Humans with wolf faces,
Seeing the names on the scraps of

Paper fluttering inside the
Jars like butterflies,
Banging against the glass,
Wanting only to live.

That's why she endured.
Why she never told them.
Nothing matters now, not medals,
Not visitors, not old labels,
"Righteous among the Nations,"

Only that they wanted to live.

Michael Shorb

FARM HORSES IN A FULL MOON

this full moon
gaining traction above
a stand of oaks,
the horses can hardly contain
themselves, like restless
children they call among shadows,
singing some tune
long ago honed in their blood,
dancing on a stage
between meadow and moon
their beauty a liquid copper
flowing in a night alive
with delights.

ENTERING THE WATER

To sit peacefully
before a log fire,
wind moaning
in the polar landscape,
to scrape a film of flies
from a washtub
of reservation water,
to have no voice
but the north coast
heron stalking
on the wind and laugh,
no voice but
the spotted bull dolphin's
tangled in the purse seine
net and laugh, no voice
but the blotched and crook-
jawed salmon after
mating on its way
to die and laugh:
       a voice of all these
animal and human forms
about to starve or fade
or be driven from the earth
       and laugh.

Recall old tribes
of the mountainous northwest,
whose young men,
       seeking visions,
climbed high buttes affording
sheer views
of blue-threaded sacred river,
and dove

ardor of the task
manifold in sweetness
of the vision.

I think of one such man,
how halfway down
an ordinary tapestry
of perfection
he saw something strange,
as through a warp
        in future distance.

I think it was us he saw.
The flash from Champlain's blunderbuss,
the Caribbe kings

driven from their parrot-
        haunted kingdoms.
The Iroquois orators and the
Rome of the Hurons
going down in self-inflicted flames.

The smallpox-stricken
Mandan vanishing from
buffalo-anointed river bluffs,
Sitting Bull shot in the back
by Sioux police, the clenched
hope of ghost dance revelers,
the congealing ice
        at Wounded Knee Creek.

He saw it sideways,
as ozone-deflected
        ultraviolet light

bounces off earth
            into space,
saw it, what was to come,
died smiling

            entering the water.

Michael Shorb

PRESIDIO CHAPEL, SAN FRANCISCO

Back up the hill
Forever safe
From the brassy
Bustle of buy and sell
Some shrined on brass
Plaques on chapel walls
Some left outside
In even rows on white stones
Ringed by a green arc
Of Eucalyptus trees
The names fading into braille
The violent colors of battle
Only notations in a book now
I wander among them
To revive my life
Brighten a faded honor
Looking toward the bay
Dotted with boats
I see the old days still
Grizzlies lumbering near
Water's edge, an air-
Borne tide of birds
All of these buildings
Nowhere to be found.

MY FATHER'S GARAGE ON CHRISTMAS NIGHT

Back after all these years
and older, the silence better,
more like friendship, two neighbors
rooting for the same team.
The rafters are filled
with the detritus
of mutual lives:
        tent we used for camping
at Big Bear Lake,
        a punching bag
nobody hits now, a sister's furniture.

Your workbench piled higher
than ever with a hundred
accomplished or forgotten
repairs and adjustments,
power sander and soldering iron askew,
a wood box filled with broken things
waiting to be renewed.

This is what you ended up with.
A garage domain
        a world of certain things,
perfect fits.
        I don't question it anymore.
Perhaps half lost
        in worlds of ideas
        and stale perplexions of beauty
I now envy this yoga of wood
and metal tightly joined
        of things
secured by bolts and industrial glue.

Once-shared, never mentioned things.

How your father took you, small boy,
down a creaking wood and wire
cage into coal mine's chambers
where a miner gave you
a perfect fish fossil
entombed on a shard of slate
from Pennsylvania's Cambrian Age.

How you smuggled corn whiskey
jugs secreted in milk cans,
running back country roads
raw winter mornings,
how you stood in your father's

corn fields dreaming of being
an aviator and washed out of flight
school in Texas after a late
night drinking binge in town.

Your genealogy project, tracing
our ancestors back to a voyage
to Baltimore aboard the Speedwell in 1762.

Admiring this platter
          you once fashioned
quail in flight
          on smoky plastic sky,
I praise it perhaps too much
or awkwardly
          meaning a hundred appreciations
left unspoken, meaning
to say you weren't what I thought
that you never understood
the anger of your sons, the drugs,
the grasping for roads—

America has nothing to do
with this. There's just the two of us,
looking more alike than
we realize, feeling
what we don't know
how to say.

HEARING LENNON'S 'IMAGINE' ON THE WRIGLEY BEACH NORTH OF MAZATLAN

In the timeless south I forgot
Draft cards and social security numbers,
In San Jose Del Pacifico
       on the mountainous
Spine of Sierra Madre below Oaxaca
I gorged on dark mushrooms packed
In jars of honey
       relishing their cobalt blue
Dots of pure psilocybin as I watched
Sudden deep green valleys undulate
Below drooling Olmec clouds heard
The brujos whirling in oxygen-
Driven rapids of my blood
Drumming a green cascade
Event horizon
       with no memory or name.

I rode the comic, pig and chicken
Laden local bus from
Puerto Angel up to Pochutla's market square,
Leaving behind only a rented cot
Straw room beach front hotel on a
Blue inlet bay, only pesos spent on
Carta Blanca and ceviche, fresh red snapper
Lanced from early morning waters,
Lobsters wrapped in giant leaves, huevos
Con salsa, small bunches of thumb-shaped
Red bananas and the shrill, brain-icing pot
Grown in the back hills by the younger fishermen.

Then coastward hitched a ride on a PRI
Road repair truck loaded with expressionless
Workers and drums of bubbling asphalt.

Walked miles alone on alien road to
Escondido Beach, stopping once to
Splash naked in a small sparkling stream
Beneath a bridge

A long ride from two Goldman
Dreamers from Idaho with antlers tied
To the front of their old panel truck
Took me through Acapulco, along wetland shallows
Thick with flocks of reddish flamingos
Rising like mist, through Guadalajara and
Up jungled coast land plain
          to Mazatlan, where vultures

Sat on the curving light poles,
Past Senor Frog's and Navigante bar
With its rope and wood bridge,
To the squatter's beach
Just south of the curving bluff and coconut
Grove on the ocean side of
The old Wrigley Mansion.

A palace built by the oral
Fixation of millions seemed,
After a few cigar-sized
Joints rolled in strips
Of newspaper and an eye-
Splitting sunset,
To be the last refuge in a world
Consumed by progress and war.

First morning a group of us,
Two women from Toronto,
A marine hitching north with his wife,
Two former tank drivers
From Danang heading

Home to somewhere east of Fairbanks
All naked, stoned in the water,
Slapping laughter
And traces of color
From the surging froth.

Walking up the beach
To gather coconuts
To mix tequila in
I heard your song,
Lennon, piped from a radio
Porch of utter clarity.

As though I had never heard a song before.

I stood there, following the dreaming flow.
If we could only stop here,
Stoned in water, laughing,
Everything stretching green
Me not returning broke to the states,
You not stretched out in awkward
Blood outside a New York street hotel,
No devil of envy shrieking,
Drugging gone bad in parody
Half Capone half
Pathogenic Peter Pan,
The measures lacking love,
Bad signs, lines
Drawn across the heart.

KINDNESS OF STRANGERS

Millions of people
I don't know
Love and care for me.
I can't turn my computer on
Without being reminded
Of their concerns.

A big shot in Nigeria
Picks me from over 300 million
Americans to share his
Uncle's fortune and I win
The UK and European lotteries
On the same day,
There are a few details.

Many people are concerned
About the size of my penis.
My inadequacy seems to be
All over cyberspace. I get
The taunting:
            "Did nature give you a big dick?"
Along with promises to
                    "Grow my man sausage by
                            Three to five inches."
I only need to send them money.

Speaking of money, there are
A thousand plans to help
Me become a millionaire
Effortlessly, sitting in my pajamas
Drinking coffee or on the deck
Of my new tropical home

Sipping rum and fruit juice.
I don't have to do a thing.
Sign a check and look in
The mail box once a day.

And I can meet a Russian bride
Or a Christian single,
Someone who will be happy to hook up
With a millionaire with a large member
With nothing to do but
Drink all day
And count his money.

I HEARD THE TREAD OF HUNTERS

I heard the tread of hunters
snapping forge
      in broken trail
across the shell-backed,
pheasant-feathered leaves
along the tracing snow-
gold waters of
October.

I heard the tread of hunters
thrashing past mossy
roots of thorn, crunching
the moldy harvest of
walnut trees.

I heard the tread of hunters
signal terror to the deer
who wandered grasslines
of clover-
breaded pools,
watched them
twitch their hate for death
and fly—

fleet hooves,
      blood and cinder
fading
      small as owls away
mandarin-delicate
flanks leaping
      in the gloom.

Michael Shorb

GALLOPING HORSE UNEARTHED
AT LEITAI, CHINA

Your blind green eyes saw all
There was to see on earth
Your massive bronze shoulders
Tested every grade
       of mineral age and snow
Chisel-stroking sunlight of creation
Motion of a vanished master's hand.

Your silence outlasted sound:
Storm where a city burned, roaring market rivers,
Carts bearing away rice, silver, human bones.

An arrogant emperor loved you more than wisdom.
Stood you running in Taoist stillness before
His palace gate, ordered a jade sparrow
Welded to your upraised hoof to show
The speed and balance of your stillness.

The cities and systems of this earth
Are wheat fields in the mind.
Grown to bearded heights of fruitfulness
They fall
       field street and armory
Threshed away
By inviolable waters of ignorant repetition.

You alone, sleeping two thousand years
Like a seed in the loam of China, remain.
I wanted to be among the Chinese diggers
Who discovered you. With a vanished
Youth bound for war who touched your hoof
For grace because he had no God.
To help hold you as the brushes strained

Residues of oblivion from your long smooth face,
Joining a common impulse
To lift you back into the blackbird-
Flooded skies of time,
Whole and human.

Michael Shorb

TUNES FOR BEARS TO DANCE TO

I took the cracked kettle
Flaubert offered me,
took it and found
two shinbones, two
sprouts from the flank
of a redwood tree,
began tapping out
tunes for bears to dance to.

The tunes traveled miles
drifting through trackless
forests like smoke,
penetrating cave and progenitor,
come out, I sang
claim love as you enter the world,
bring your sturdy paws
and your need to dance,
we'll dig up the dented horn
and the old violin someone
buried by the river,
we'll find a meadow
bathed in moonlight and
darting with fireflies,
there

      with each lurching
step we can begin
the world again.

AHURA MAZDA

This sand and thistle
wilderness once held
gardens where we greeted
fighting Cambyses home
from Egyptian conquest
with slaves, ivory, gold,
a stable of captured gods.

We feasted, glittering
        dancers whirled
Priests of Ahura Mazda
filled our cups
with liquid glory.

Waking, we find the city under siege.
Macedonian javelins raining down,
runners bawling out the dread
from Granicus. There's a new god now,
Aristotle's prize student,
        Alexander Mastodon
a phalanx of bloody
dust spilling into Asia
Egypt India
        like a plague.

Our survey indicates a finite
number of horsehide insect whisks
Nubian slaves loading bales
        of colored cotton
tusks, spices, pottery
precious stones and bulging
granaries, newly-erected temples.
Then it darkens
        armies roll,

locusts drizzle through
river orchards, illuminated
manuscripts go for fish wrap.

Each human's got a part to play.

I was the grinning wanderer who
played the flute or juggled
green bottles in torchlit courtyards,
I was the plain man with
        the shriveled belly,
a bricklayer, a sail maker,
the man who buried fallen legions
with balm and special markings
        coins lidding the eyes.
This process, profit and loss,
began with dried
        fish and carved elk horn,
flints and surgery exchanged for
water in summer
        salt in winter.

Who knows if anything ever dies?

Fall off a Turkish siege ladder at
Constantinople into a dark vortex
of smoking emptiness
        and points
of echoing fire,
see what happens then.

        A last memory
will be the full yellow moon
a woman's touch
the smile of a friend.

The ideas we know about.
They're always around
shuffled from fleet to caravan
maybe getting less attention by now
being laughed at, ridiculed,
abused in the marketplace.

You simply make less impression
each time you exist.
      Begin as a god
deep in the velvet
      myths of Persia if you must,
you'll end up propping
open a temple door
      in the seedy part of town,
naming a rotary engine
automobile by the time
the 20th Century rolls.

An excellent system
come to think of it.
Natural selection
      among archetypes.
Each vehicle becoming its own
      model of the universe
complete with ritualized
accessories
      customized concepts
of duty and freedom.

Me, I love my new
Olympus XL Grand Operatic
camper with dashboard pantheon
sacred bough orphic stereo tape deck
barbed wire doors, food, fuel and liquor

ensuring our survival, yours
in the abstract sense
        mine in the concrete sense.

In this vehicle there is nothing to fear.
One recent evening I ploughed through
a mob of irate campesinos
while driving west on the Trans-Amazon Highway.

In my spotlights they scattered,
buzzing and bristling in the manner
of the starving, gnashing their
teeth as the weight of my place
in this night—
        the only man for miles around
with liquor and food, dawned on them.

Driving on, I caught a glimpse
of a Roman legion lost in
the Sahara of my rear view mirror,
or extinct deer grazing
        in a dammed-up canyon.

Now is the perfect time.
My god and I light up a
Cuban cigar, open a bottle of
'46 Bordeaux, the magic radio
comes on with mankind's
greatest hits:
        Roland's horn, Oppenheimer's
mushrooming parody of Mozart's
magic flute caress the steaming,
bird-infested darkness.

Now you will hear a music
that does not dream
of what is past or passing, or to come.
Roll up the window
to block out the annoying
vegetable tides.

Listen.

UNCLE STERRY

This old house, set off the road
to Valley Falls, aged to
birch white and peeling
like shingled skin, this mapled
driveway
       lost in autumnal hues,
clay-stained leaves
running wild in antlered sun.

A strong man, neighbors called him.
Good as any ever wore
a pair of shoes.

       But now, with his wife
living in town
       nursing a broken ankle,
TV glows and drones,
blue parody of the burning bush, as we
approach the door.

The homogenized babble of talking heads
looms incongruous here
in Rockwell country:

       any voice to fill
the twilight now,
       any mode of sleep.

We talk of the madness of California weather.

"All the same son, day after day.
No seasons. Like a neon tube.
Must confuse animals. With animals
you need seasons.
       Rain snow.

The exact gold of October.
There's a time to rest the mare and a time
to foal.
          The same with sheep, and cows."

The only thing he regrets, says Uncle Sterry,
is giving up his car
          because of cataracts.
That, and letting his delicate wife
Blanche sleep alone by the dining
room heater the night
she rose from troubled
sleep and stepped
          through a closed glass
door toward the warmth
of relatives in town.

As evening wears on
Uncle Sterry reveals
ghosts and skeletons
of apple butter country.
The Irishman
          crazed by debts and whiskey
who bludgeoned his wife and two boys
burying them beneath flat rocks
in a field of stubbled corn.

"Or you take the Millers now.
Stu and Aurelia? She had
that slight hunch back, don't you know.
Hadn't oughtta had no children, them two.
Six kids born.
Three was normal. Three was dwarfs.
Hadn't oughtta
          had no children."

The time to depart grows like a shadow.

We say goodbye to
Uncle Sterry
  shaking those burled hands
that once milked and sowed and
baled hay in the course of morning.

I don't even know what I felt
driving back
  light beams cutting
the air like molten snow.

A loss.

Not sorrow exactly
but cheated
  and a fear.

AFTER A PEARL HARBOR IN CYBERSPACE

First I wake up
in someone else's skin,
I'm a Chinese or Brazilian
consumer today, my stock
portfolio's erased, I'm reduced
to relying on gold bars
and parking meter change,
an armed guard at
my front door demands
who I am and why
I wear the stolen winged
shoes of Mercury
lifted from the excavation site,
where the discovery of
broken bones and shards
of pottery exceeds all expectations,
still searching for my birth
certificate and dna analysis,
I'm sternly informed
if I don't understand the language
pouring from my television,
I am to report immediately
to a terminal beyond
the oil fields, where the last days
are canceled
          until further envelopment,
and the contents of my mind
hereby both digitized
and privatized for my own protection,
leaving me only the mineral rights
to my own memories,
which I will quickly
barter away.

A POSTCARD LIFE OF GERONIMO

The wheels run, even in sleep.

Pictures: (1858) the fair Alope scalped,
Eyes spooned out by bounty-seeking
Mexican irregulars; you had no purpose
Left then, remains of a first wife and three
Daughters burning like fireweed on charred ground
Words formed: Revenge All The Time.
15 years of raids looming through dust ambushed
Ranchers shot in startled faces, horses and cattle
Stolen, retreats into the sheltering Mexican
Mountains
      Sierra Madre
War Mother pursued peak by peak by the slow
Blues on heavy horses,
The 25-mile-a-day
Representatives of Manifest Destiny.

Pictures: (1884) surrendering and the march
To foul San Carlos, even the agents called it
"Hell's 40 Acres," 110 degrees in summer shade,
Beset by a million nameless bugs, fed by the thieves
Of the "Tucson Ring" who brought wobbling
Cattle bony as thorns.
      Sinking into miasma of torpid
Afternoons broken only by wife-
Beating gambling and corn-
Mash tiswin drunks, spied on by turncoat scouts:
Proud Mickey Free and Dutchy, who proved his
Mettle by hunting down and beheading his own father
For the murder of a white man.

Pictures: (1885) escape again, the mountains below
Imaginary borders looming like freedom, making false
Camps, going seventy miles a day, setting fires to
Make the following enemy ride through fire.
What life but a trail of blood, in and out of
The Chiricahua Mountains, tracks covered
By blinding snow, in 90 days you rolled
1200 miles, killed 38 people, stole 250
Horses and mules, left behind a relic
Of the Charred ground inside you became a name for
Death and hard riding, alternative
to Ghost Dancing.

The wheels run even in sleep.

Pictures: (1886) 440 men women children of
A mountain race loaded into boxcars sent
Along with the Apache scouts who tracked you
From Fort Apache to Fort Pickens, Florida damp
Lowland ground and hard labor sawing logs
Many died there or at Mount Vernon Barracks,
Alabama, then relative mercy of Fort Sill
Oklahoma and the white man's road, inept
Raiser of hogs but good with turkeys and chickens.
Preacher at a Dutch Reformed Church Sunday school,
Master of a fair-sized patch of watermelons.

Pictures: (1904) this the Age of Marketing.
The photographers come, posing you with dusty
Watermelons, crouching with trademark scowl
And empty Sharp's rifle.
        By permission of War Department
You become a showman, wild west clown decked in warrior
Drag at St. Louis World's Fair.
The 'attraction' Geronimo
The poster man Geronimo

Maker of souvenir arrows bows Geronimo
Hired for one year stint by wild west show
White man's money
White man's whiskey
White man's writing 'GERONIMO' in block letters
White man's clothes in boy's sized
Battered suitcase.

"Even now there is a fire in the old man's eyes."
Wrote Washington DC interviewer
When he recalls the raids of his youth
The riding into light on stolen horses.

Pictures: (1909) they say he slipped off his horse
Coming from town drunk and talking to himself
Raving about forgiveness, Arizona
That he lay face up in the rain
Calling a name: "Alope"
That more than age or pneumonia killed the warrior:

February 17, 1909

The wheels run, even in sleep.

THE LOST NOVELS OF
WILLIAM SHAKESPEARE

When it comes to
history we don't know
much, always
gleaners trodding
harvested fields,
combing rubble,
we know most of
Sophocles' plays
were lost, are happy
with the two books
salvaged from the work
of Homer, don't even
know the story of how
the novels of the glove-
maker's son were lost,
consigned to flames.

Clocked out after
writing scripts in
London, he came
back to country ways,
petty business deals, sunsets.
He tired of the stage,
grew bored with the cross-
word clockworks of the sonnet.
None knew his midnight thoughts,
how he dreamed again, a long work,
all soliloquy, the last thoughts
and life story of the Catholic
heretic he'd seen burned alive

as a boy, a single sentence,
200 pages long.

Lear's tale told by his fool was next.

And, centuries before Joyce,
Shylock's story unadorned,
a Jew in Venice running
stations of the double cross,
the history of the world
woven into the background.

Last of all the details:
a chest of papers
discovered after death,
an erstwhile business partner
bearing a grudge who
cleaned out the great man's house,
that moment frozen in time,
as he lifts the chest over
his head, heaving it
into a pile of soiled linen
and broken wood
smoldering in wait.

COAL MINE CANARIES

We are all this thick-
armed man covered in soot,
placing nature in his
cage as he descends,
miles into the darkening
shaft of our prospects,
now the honey bee is enlisted
to our cause, billions
vanished without trace
or clue, bearing with them
the keys to pollination,
something gone wrong
in the intricate corridors
of seeds and blossoms,
next the plankton
roots that rock
the cradle of the seas,
the icy arctic walls holding
back a methane storm,
the salt water hordes
massing at the granite
gates where we make
our stand, man
the miner,
man the harvester,
man more vulnerable
than he dreams.

Michael Shorb

KARMAGEDDON

we should have known
the way of the west
was doomed to evolve
into a single planetary
traffic jam, anyway we're stuck,
the wheel don't spin,
ironic we should all be homeless now,
thank god for A/C and iPhones,
those on the way to the tailgate party
become the new upper class
even as all remaining games are canceled,
and our collective thoughts,
in the reddening portals of night,
turn toward food.

THE IMPOSSIBILITY OF PRAYER

I mistook it for God—

vast vacant black
punctuated by blizzards of
dying stars—

A tribute to
          how small I felt,
And how alone.

What was I doing here,
on the banks of this
rivered eternity?

The stumbling cycles
of my life
amount to nothing,
a trillion atoms
forming the shadow
of a drop of rain.

Michael Shorb

CHERNOBYL SPRING

in gray and yellow woods
just beyond reach
of the sealed-off cement
and metal behemoth
left behind

the eager allure of birdsong
catches at your heart,
tugs the dazzled legs of your trousers,
"come on" the plea
reaches your genes in a breath,
balances hope on the note
forward, the implied normalcy
of tenderness, the feathers extended

allow me to join my lament,
weaving into it the gradual,
sickening realization
that 99% of these birds are male,
that nature's feminine's
been strip-mined, driven into ditches

left with a hole in her wing
and no fair chance to sail,
she hesitates, hearing your
love songs and liking them well enough,
but return to those woods
in these scant times?

Walk past the way things were cheated,
when a net broke
and something shadowed
the other voice of rain.

MORE THAN THE END OF COUNTING

(For Judith)

I will die
when the time comes,
I will change
the grains in
appropriate snow,
folding solids
into stem, watching
gates of the lobe
burst as the engine
of the heart silences
churn and sparkle
of running blood.

Just now though,
while breath delights
my tongue and the unflawed
beads of summer cluster
at my eyes, I would rather
spend the afternoon
touching your face
than journey to the source
of greenwood,
   I would
rather watch you
turning
   in your
sleep than explore

the stars.

THERE MUST BE THE THINGS OF BEAUTY

In a walled garden, roses of the copper baron
Bloom, a portrait of the meat packer's
Queen's on the wall, even the sharkskin
Senator's got a diamond stickpin.

And the ship in the vault with a
Canceled blue sail's worth
half a million.

African slaves and
       Arabian Horses
Wobble down a wharf alive
With caged yellow and green macaws
Coiled ropes of pearl
Bananas, mangoes, spices.

Somewhere there is one stag amber
Antlers thrown back out of rifle range
One whale with its ploughing jaw
Has evaded the spearing lanes.
       We are immigrants brazen
Dancers holding each other in waning
Heat and light, marching down spring-
Gorged meadows to kill plant and pray.

Even the blackened throat of the cave
Will bear the harvester's pigment, a bead
Slipping through time. These orchards
After rain might be anywhere on earth
This grain a lake, this morning with its
Necklace of sleeping owls a final one
For fear and hunger.

If you don't have a death song
make one up.
>Only the brightest
>salmon remain

in midair
>leaping.

THE ROMAN SOLDIER'S EAR

No one ever talks about
the Roman soldier's ear
in the midnight garden
when they arrested rebel
Jesus and an angry
early Christian sliced off
the ear of one of the soldiers
and it plummeted to the dust
throbbing and bloody something from
a Bosch nightmare painting
and the guy's bleeding and this raw
gash on the side of his head is stinging
like ants then smoothly as a ship's
sail in a rising wind this soft-
eyed guy reaches down
picks up the ear and reattaches it
effortlessly and cool blue water
runs through the soldier's head and everything's
absolutely normal they go on with
the arrest and beat and crucify
the miracle worker anyway—

you must wonder though:
didn't the soldiers talk about it?
They weren't amazed and nobody said
maybe this guy's a wizard or a god
don't mess with him or why nobody
told Pilate about it so he could have
set him up with a night club in
Rome and had him perform
tricks like Moses turning
sticks into vipers or
water into blood?

They just went on with the crucifixion
and the soldier from time to time would feel his ear
and think to himself:
"I can't believe that happened."

THE DOLPHIN MESSENGER

Late afternoon and flawed sea unfurling
Wave on wave, diminishing sun
Sculpting copper roads of light on wet sand.
Walking, I came upon a beached dolphin
Battered by sand and the beaks of gulls.
First urged myself to walk on, avoiding
Dead things with white bellies mottled
Black by wind and talon. Not stare
At the zero of its stillness, blood
Tugging water washed from a hole
In its head, or touch the rubbery beauty
Of its lifeless fins, or marvel
At the jade serenity gracing its delicate
Mouth, the coral hues asleep there.

For I have never seen a richer smile
On friend or lover's face than this
The gangster of the sea gave back
So carelessly to the solar bell
Mushrooming on the dark water.

A wave came spattering around my ankles,
Reminding me that the sea had business
Here with one of its own, that no rituals
Shrined the reality of drying blood,
No Dolphin Father loomed and no songs sounded.

I kept walking, day used up, dreaming
A human love not of the sea
Or its shining casualties,
Guided by what seemed
An echo of the first unwrinkling stars,
Memory beyond memory, a dolphin's
Void and engulfing smile.

www.ingramcontent.com/pod-product-compliance
Lightning Source LLC
LaVergne TN
LVHW091311080426
835510LV00007B/465